SUMMARY OF PROPHETS, POLITICS AND NATIONS

Understanding the Vital Role that Prophetic Voices Play in Shaping History

EMMA STARK

D DESTINY IMAGE

Destiny Image P.O. Box 310, Shippensburg, PA 17257-0310

This book and all other Destiny Image's books are available at
Christian bookstores and distributors worldwide.

For Worldwide Distribution.

Reach us on the Internet: www.destinyimage.com.

ISBN 13 TP: 9780768483918

ISBN 13 eBook: 9780768483925

CONTENTS

CONTENTS

INTRODUCTION

☙❧☙

This book serves as a vital resource for Christians navigating the complex intersections of faith, politics, and societal responsibilities. In a world increasingly characterized by polarization and ideological extremes, it offers a clarion call for believers to embody the principles of the Kingdom of God amidst earthly governance systems. Drawing from biblical narratives, contemporary theological insights, and practical guidance, the book challenges readers to critically evaluate their political engagements, prophetic utterances, and cultural biases through the lens of Scripture.

By exploring the roles of prophets and believers in various political and cultural settings, "Summary of Prophets, Politics, and Nations" provides a comprehensive framework for understanding how divine principles should influence Christian behavior in public arenas. It advocates for a balanced approach that neither retreats from the world nor conforms to its patterns, encouraging a prophetic voice that speaks truth to power while upholding Christ's teachings of love, justice, and mercy. This introduction sets the stage for a deeper exploration into how Christians can effectively participate in building God's Kingdom on Earth, ensuring their actions reflect their ultimate allegiance to God's sovereignty and redemptive plan.

GOD SHAKES THE WORLD

Bible Verse

"For thus says the Lord of hosts: 'Once more (it is a little while) I will shake heaven and earth, the sea and dry land;'" - Haggai 2:6 (NKJV)

Introduction

I n "God Shakes the World," the author explores the divine purpose behind God's great shakings of the world, aligning current global tumults with biblical prophecy. Through profound scriptural insights and contemporary observations, the chapter emphasizes the necessity of understanding God's timing and the redemptive intentions behind His fearsome actions.

Word of Wisdom

"God is harvest-orientated and puts thornbushes in our path, so we stretch to find Him." Emma Stark

Main Theme

The chapter delves into the prophetic significance of global upheavals, arguing that God uses these dramatic events to awaken humanity to His presence and to guide us towards redemption, urging a deeper understanding of the spiritual and prophetic timings of these events.

Key Points

- God's actions in shaking the world are part of a divine strategy to provoke humanity toward decisions that align with His will.
- Significant global events, like widespread elections and natural disasters, are seen as manifestations of God's shaking.
- The concept of freedom is critically examined, contrasting worldly definitions with the true freedom found in Jesus Christ.
- False idols and human-made systems are highlighted as inadequate in the face of God's overwhelming power and judgment.
- Prophetic insights suggest that current global alliances and political structures will be tested and found wanting.
- The call for Christian leaders to redefine freedom and offer hope in a tumultuous world is emphasized.

Key Themes

- • **Divine Timing and Prophecy**: The chapter underscores the importance of recognizing God's sovereign timing in the midst of global crises. It suggests that understanding the "rhythms of Heaven" is crucial for interpreting the times and responding appropriately to God's call.

- **Redemptive Purpose of Divine Shakings**: By invoking powerful translations of Isaiah, the author illustrates that God's intention to shake the earth is not random but aimed at redemption. Each shaking is a call to awaken and realign with God's purposes, urging humanity to seek refuge in Jesus.

- **Global Political and Natural Upheavals**: Discussing the "year of the vote" and subsequent political and natural calamities, the chapter connects these events to biblical prophecies about end times, presenting them as clear signs of God's active presence in world affairs.

- **Crisis of Modern Freedom**: A deep dive into the concept of freedom shows how contemporary interpretations often stray from biblical truth. The author challenges these notions by presenting a Kingdom-centered definition of freedom, rooted in being free from sin and resembling Christ.

- **Failure of Human Systems**: Highlighting the inevitable downfall of human-made idols and systems, the text argues that reliance on such structures will lead to disappointment. It stresses the need for a foundation built on divine rather than human principles.

- **Prophetic Leadership and Communication**: The necessity for

Christian leaders to speak with clarity and hope in an era of confusion is stressed. Leaders are called to transcend church boundaries and engage with the world by defining true freedom and offering biblical solutions.

Conclusion

"God Shakes the World" serves as a clarion call for believers to discern the times, understand the deeper spiritual implications of global events, and respond with a Christ-centered perspective. It reminds us that through every shaking, God is directing us towards a future where His Kingdom reigns supreme.

CHAPTER 2

WAR AND HARVEST

Bible Verse

"For the Lord is a God of justice; blessed are all
those who wait for Him." - Isaiah 30:18 (NKJV)

Introduction

"**W**ar and Harvest" critically examines
the concept of just war and the role
of divine justice in conflicts, emphasizing the need for a prophetic understanding of
wars and the redemptive opportunities they
present. The author urges believers to seek God's
perspective on conflicts and to engage in spiritual
warfare that aligns with God's purposes of salvation
and redemption.

Word of Wisdom

*"We must only see what is happening
within the context of mass harvest and
salvations." Emma Stark*

Main Theme

This chapter explores the complex relationship between divine justice, human conflict, and the overarching goal of spiritual harvest. It discusses how believers should respond to global conflicts, not merely as spectators but as active participants in God's redemptive plan through prayer and evangelism.

Key Points

- God disapproves of excessive violence in wars, emphasizing justice even during conflict.
- Conflicts should be viewed as opportunities for spiritual harvest and salvation.
- Believers are called to engage in spiritual warfare against ideologies that foster hate and division.
- Evangelism and soul-winning are crucial in times of global upheaval.
- The resurgence of extremist ideologies like fascism needs to be countered with the gospel.

Key Themes

- **Divine Disapproval of Excessive Violence**: The author points out that God's wrath is kindled against nations that engage in unjust violence, referencing biblical narratives where God chastises His own people for overreaching in warfare. This establishes a clear divine stance against excessive and unjust violence in conflicts.

- **Redemptive View of Global Conflicts**: Conflicts are not just disruptions; they are seen as divinely allowed circumstances that can lead to significant spiritual outcomes. The turmoil of wars shakes people from complacency, making them more receptive to the gospel, which believers should capitalize on.

- **Role of the Church in Modern Conflicts**: The church is called to be a prophetic voice against the rising tide of extremist ideologies like fascism. It should actively oppose any form of ideology that promotes discrimination and violence, using biblical principles as its foundation.

- **Importance of Evangelism in Times of Crisis**: The chapter underscores the necessity for believers to intensify their evangelistic efforts during global crises. It is a time for the church to fulfill its calling by turning these crises into harvest fields, bringing many to Christ.

- **Spiritual Warfare and Prophetic Insight**: Believers are urged to understand and engage in spiritual warfare, not only against spiritual wickedness but also against the ideologies and systemic evils that underpin much of the world's conflict today.

Conclusion

"War and Harvest" calls for a profound engagement with the complexities of war from a Christian perspective that prioritizes justice, redemption, and evangelism. The chapter challenges believers to rise above the conventional views on war and engage actively in God's redemptive mission during these tumultuous times. The future of global evangelism and the effectiveness of the church's response to war hinge on our willingness to embrace this prophetic and redemptive perspective.

CHAPTER 3

WARTIME PROPHETS AND SATAN'S STRATEGY

Bible Verse

"Behold, I have given you authority to tread on serpents and scorpions, and over all the power of the enemy, and nothing shall hurt you." - Luke 10:19 (ESV)

Introduction

In "Wartime Prophets and Satan's Strategy," the focus is on the critical role of prophetic voices during times of global crisis. This chapter unpacks how God raises prophetic leaders to guide His people, contrasted with Satan's tactics to derail God's plan.

Word of Wisdom

"When a nation is in crisis, God always sends them a prophetic voice."
Emma Stark

Main Theme

The chapter delves into the dynamics of spiritual warfare, emphasizing the importance of the prophetic ministry in interpreting and combating the spiritual challenges of our time. It portrays the prophetic community as essential in navigating and countering Satan's strategies during wartime.

Key Points

- God appoints prophets to lead and offer divine insights during crises.
- The prophetic role involves both declaring God's truth and combating Satan's lies.
- Accusations and spiritual exhaustion are primary tactics used by Satan against believers.
- Prophetic voices are vital in maintaining the timing and purity of divine messages.
- The end-times church is depicted as powerful, with the ability to perform miraculous acts as God's witnesses.

Key Themes

- **Prophetic Leadership in Crisis**: The chapter emphasizes that during national or global crises, God specifically raises prophetic voices to guide His people. These prophets are not only messengers but also warriors in spiritual battles, equipped to handle divine revelations and deliver them amidst adversity.

- **Satan's Tactics Against Prophets**: Satan's strategy includes accusations, creating exhaustion, and distorting God's timing to weaken the prophets' impact. This theme explores how these tactics aim to disrupt the spiritual authority of God's chosen leaders and the broader church's effectiveness.

- **Preservation and Purity of Prophetic Voices**: It's highlighted that God prepares and preserves His prophetic people to stay pure and unaffected by Satan's attacks. This purification process ensures that their declarations remain untainted and powerful, aligning perfectly with God's timing.

- **Role of Prophets in Spiritual Warfare**: The text outlines the prophets' role in spiritual warfare, stressing that they battle not just with words but through divine authority that can alter natural elements and societal structures according to God's will.

- **Impact of End-Times Prophetic Ministry**: The prophetic ministry in the end times is marked by miraculous powers akin to those of biblical figures like Moses and Elijah. This indicates an escalation in spiritual authority as the age draws to a close, positioning the church to confront and conquer the growing darkness.

Conclusion

"Wartime Prophets and Satan's Strategy" offers a profound insight into the essential role of prophetic voices in spiritual warfare, especially in times of conflict. The chapter encourages believers to understand and support the prophetic ministry, recognizing its crucial role in God's redemptive plan during turbulent times. It calls for a vigilant and spiritually active church, prepared to both declare and demonstrate the kingdom of God against the backdrop of Satan's opposing forces.

CHAPTER 4

KINGDOM-THINKING CITIZENS

Bible Verse

"But seek first the kingdom of God and His righteousness, and all these things shall be added to you." - Matthew 6:33 (NKJV)

Introduction

In "Kingdom-Thinking Citizens," the narrative centers on the transformative role of Christians as agents of the Kingdom of God, contrasting this with the often reactionary and protective tendencies of the contemporary church. The chapter highlights the need for believers to operate with a revolutionary mindset, driven by Kingdom principles rather than worldly concerns.

Word of Wisdom

"Perhaps those of us who claimed to prophesy have been living more as citizens of the world than of Heaven, preoccupied

with our own nations rather than capti-vated by the Kingdom of God." Emma Stark

Main Theme

This chapter discusses the critical importance of aligning our thoughts and actions with the Kingdom of God, especially in turbulent times. It challenges Christians to rethink their roles as passive observers and to become proactive, revolutionary forerunners of God's transformative power on earth.

Key Points

• The Kingdom of God (KOG) is a spiritual realm that coexists with our world, influencing and transforming it.

• Jesus inaugurated the KOG, which continues to expand through signs, wonders, and the actions of believers.

• Believers are called to be revolutionary forerunners, moving beyond mere maintenance of church norms to actively shaping the future with Kingdom values.

• Prophetic voices in the church must emanate from Kingdom reality, not worldly perspectives.

• Christians are urged to let go of defensive and reactionary tendencies, embracing a forward-thinking, transformative approach.

Key Themes

- **Nature and Expansion of the Kingdom of God**: The Kingdom of God is depicted not just as a future promise but as a present reality, initiated by Jesus and expanding through the church's engagement with the world. This Kingdom is dynamic, marked by miraculous signs and an ongoing battle against evil forces.
- **Role of Believers as Revolutionary Forerunners**: Christians are envisioned as agents who anticipate and catalyze divine action in the world. Moving away from a defensive posture, they are to engage actively in manifesting God's Kingdom through bold, transformative actions and prophetic declarations.
- **Misalignment of Prophetic Voices with Kingdom Values**: There is a critical examination of how prophetic voices have often been tainted by worldly allegiances rather than Kingdom priorities. This misalignment leads to distorted perceptions and ineffective ministry, hindering the church's mission.
- **Transformation of Church Identity and Mission**: The chapter calls for a fundamental transformation in the church's self-understanding and mission. It emphasizes transitioning from an institution that often mirrors worldly structures and values to one that robustly embodies and advances Kingdom principles.

- **Practical Steps for Living as Kingdom-Thinking Citizens**: Believers are encouraged to adopt a mindset that prioritizes God's Kingdom over earthly concerns, including nationalistic or personal agendas. This involves a deep, personal commitment to seeking God's will and a readiness to act as His agents of change in every sphere of life.

Conclusion

"Kingdom-Thinking Citizens" serves as a rallying cry for believers to embrace their identity as active participants in God's Kingdom. The chapter implores Christians to shift their focus from internal church politics and worldly concerns to the transformative and expansive nature of the Kingdom of God. By adopting this mindset, believers can effectively influence their surroundings and contribute to a global manifestation of God's reign on earth.

CHAPTER 5

BIBLICAL NATIONHOOD

Bible Verse

"From one man he made all the nations, that they should inhabit the whole earth; and he marked out their appointed times in history and the boundaries of their lands." - Acts 17:26 (NIV)

Introduction

"Biblical Nationhood" explores how God views nations according to the Bible, emphasizing the distinction between biblical nationalism and biblical nationhood. The chapter highlights how God uses nations to reflect His character and purposes, shaping their identities and destinies according to His divine plan.

Word of Wisdom

"A nation usually gets the leader it deserves." Emma Stark

Main Theme

This chapter delves into the concept of nations as entities established by God with distinct identities and purposes. It discusses how nations are instrumental in God's plan, each displaying unique aspects of His character and contributing to the global understanding of His nature.

Key Points

• God establishes nations with specific boundaries and identities.

• Nations are meant to lead people to seek and find God.

• Each nation reflects unique attributes of God's character.

• God determines the rise and fall of nations according to His purposes.

• Believers are encouraged to appreciate and learn from the diversity of nations.

Key Themes

• **Divine Purpose in National Boundaries**: The chapter explains that God has designed nations with specific boundaries and times, intending for these divisions to help people seek Him. This design is not accidental but a strategic part of His missiological plan to reveal Himself to humanity through diverse national characteristics.

- **Role of Nations in God's Plan**: Each nation, according to the chapter, is endowed with unique attributes that reflect different aspects of God's character. This diversity means that every nation can teach us something about God, emphasizing the importance of cross-cultural respect and learning.
- **God's Sovereignty Over National Destinies**: The rise and fall of nations are portrayed as acts of divine sovereignty, where God blesses nations to display His glory or diminishes them as a form of judgment. This theme challenges the perception of historical and political power as purely human endeavors.
- **Prophetic Insight into National Leadership**: The chapter suggests that the quality of national leadership can be a sign of God's favor or disfavor. Prophetic discernment is needed to understand whether leaders are being raised up or diminished by God as part of His judgment on nations.
- **Cultural and Ethical Reflections of God in Nations**: It is posited that every cultural expression and national characteristic can reflect God's nature. Believers are encouraged to discern and celebrate how God's attributes are uniquely manifested in their own and other cultures.

Conclusion

"Biblical Nationhood" provides a profound theological framework for understanding the role and significance of nations in God's divine plan. By recognizing the unique ways in which nations reflect God's glory and serve His purposes, believers can better appreciate the divine orchestration of history and cultural diversity. This perspective not only enriches faith but also fosters a more respectful and curious approach to international and intercultural relations.

CHAPTER 6

THE BEAUTY OF
YOUR RACE

Bible Verse

"From one man he made all nations to inhabit the
whole earth, and he allotted the times of their
existence and the boundaries of the places where
they would live, so that they would search for God
and perhaps grope for him and find him—though
indeed he is not far from any one of us." - Acts
17:26 (NRSVUE)

Introduction

"The Beauty of Your Race" explores the
profound connection between racial diversity and the character of God. It emphasizes that every racial attribute, from skin color
to facial features, is a unique reflection of God's
image, designed to teach us about His character
and to foster unity among His creation.

Word of Wisdom

"No race, according to Acts 17:26-28, is superior. No nationality should consider itself the cream of humanity, or the best representative of the Kingdom of God."

Main Theme

This chapter discusses the biblical view of race, highlighting that racial diversity is God's design and serves a divine purpose. It counters the notions of racial superiority and promotes the understanding that all humans are created in the image of God, offering diverse reflections of His nature.

Key Points

• Every race reflects unique aspects of God's character.

• Racial diversity is intended to lead us to a greater understanding of God.

• Scripture rejects racial superiority and promotes unity.

• The fallen characteristics of nations or races are not indicative of God's design.

• Cross-racial understanding and marriages enrich our comprehension of God.

Key Themes

- **Theological Basis for Racial Diversity**: The chapter establishes that racial diversity is rooted in the creation of humanity from one blood, underscoring that all humans reflect God's image. This theological foundation challenges and refutes any basis for racial discrimination or superiority.

- **Racial Attributes as Reflections of God**: It explains how different racial features, such as skin color and facial structures, are expressions of God's creativity and diversity. Each race brings a unique perspective on God's character, enriching our collective understanding of who God is.

- **The Impact of Sin on Racial Perceptions**: Sin has distorted how races perceive one another, leading to stereotypes and prejudices that mar the image of God in humanity. The chapter calls for a reexamination of these fallen characteristics through a biblical lens, promoting a return to God's original intent for diversity.

- **Globalization and Biblical Nationhood**: While addressing globalization, the text emphasizes that the Bible does not support a homogenized global identity but cherishes the distinctiveness of each nation and race. This diversity is seen as a way to fully display the manifold nature of God's kingdom on earth.

- **Future Unity in Diversity**: The ultimate gathering of all races and nations before God, as depicted in Revelation, illustrates the eschatological vision of unity. This unity does not erase racial distinctions but celebrates them as part of God's eternal kingdom.

Conclusion

"The Beauty of Your Race" reaffirms that every human being is a unique expression of the divine image. It calls for Christians to recognize and celebrate racial diversity as a divine gift meant to enrich our understanding of God and to promote unity within the body of Christ. By embracing this biblical perspective, believers are encouraged to actively reject racism and to honor the dignity and worth of every race and ethnicity.

CHAPTER 7

THE DANGER OF
EXTREME NATIONALISM

Bible Verse

"Watch out for the yeast of the Pharisees and that
of Herod." - Mark 8:15 (NIV)

Introduction

The Danger of Extreme Nationalism"
explores the hazardous implications of
excessive national pride that escalates
into idolatry. This chapter critiques how nationalism can distort the church's mission and the
Christian's view of God's kingdom, urging caution
especially for prophetic figures within the church.

Word of Wisdom

*"Warning! Extreme Nationalism is
especially dangerous ground for prophets
and prophetic people to step onto!" Emma
Stark*

Main Theme

The chapter delves into how extreme nationalism can compromise the integrity of the Christian message by aligning it too closely with political and nationalistic goals, potentially leading to idolatry and a departure from biblical truths.

Key Points

• Extreme nationalism idolizes national identity, often at the cost of external inclusivity.

• It has historically been associated with xenophobia and the demonization of political and cultural enemies.

• Christian leaders must be wary of aligning too closely with nationalistic movements that could distort the gospel.

• Nationalism can distract Christians from their primary identity and mission in Christ.

• The church must remain vigilant against the seductive power of political ideologies masquerading as religious fervor.

Key Themes

• **Dangers to Prophetic Integrity**:
  Prophets and prophetic people are at risk of losing their divine focus when they engage too deeply in nationalist ideologies, which can lead to a distortion of their messages and a potential fall into idolatry. This chapter cautions against the lure of

aligning prophetic messages with nationalistic agendas that prioritize political objectives over spiritual truths.

- **Historical Warnings and Contemporary Implications**: Reflecting on the historical misuse of Christianity to endorse extreme nationalist agendas, the chapter draws parallels to contemporary issues where nationalistic fervor often co-opts religious rhetoric. This blending poses significant risks to the church's mission and can undermine its prophetic voice in society.
- **Impact on Church Mission and Identity**: The entanglement of nationalism and Christianity can lead the church to stray from its mission, focusing more on political victories than on spiritual growth and discipleship. The chapter challenges churches to reassess their priorities and the influence of nationalism on their practices and teachings.
- **Biblical Perspective on Nations and Kingdoms**: By contrasting the biblical view of nations with the often idolatrous nature of nationalism, the chapter emphasizes that while patriotism can be healthy, it becomes problematic when it overshadows or contradicts the principles of God's kingdom. It discusses how the New Testament shifts the focus from territorial to spiritual kingdom-building.
- **Call to Prophetic and Pastoral Responsibility**: Leaders are urged to critically evaluate their engagement with nationalism and to shepherd their

congregations toward a kingdom-oriented perspective that transcends political and national allegiances. This involves a recommitment to the gospel's transcultural and transnational message.

Conclusion

"The Danger of Extreme Nationalism" serves as a sobering reminder of the perils of allowing nationalistic fervor to dictate the church's agenda. It calls for a reevaluation of how deeply the church and its leaders are intertwined with national identities and political ambitions. By refocusing on the Kingdom of God, Christians can maintain a prophetic witness that speaks truth to power while transcending the divisive and often destructive currents of extreme nationalism.

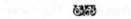

CHAPTER 8

PATRIOTISM VERSUS EXTREME NATIONALISM

Bible Verse

"But seek first the kingdom of God and His righteousness, and all these things shall be added to you." —Matthew 6:33 (NKJV)

Introduction

"Patriotism Versus Extreme Nationalism" differentiates between healthy patriotism and the dangers of extreme nationalism. This chapter examines how an exaggerated sense of national pride can lead to idolatry, where the nation itself is revered above God's Kingdom, distorting the Christian's mission and allegiance.

Word of Wisdom

"Nationalism is patriotism gone wrong. Nationalism grows out of misplaced patriotism." Emma Stark

Main Theme

The chapter discusses the importance of maintaining a balanced perspective on national identity within the Christian faith. It warns against allowing patriotism to evolve into nationalism, which can eclipse the primary focus on God's Kingdom and distort Christian witness.

Key Points

• Patriotism should be present but not dominant in a Christian's life.

• Extreme nationalism idolizes national identity, often at God's expense.

• It can lead to a superiority complex and conflict.

• Nationalism within borders can foster divisiveness and tribalism.

• The church must guard against becoming unteachable and overly nationalistic.

Key Themes

• **Misplaced Priorities Leading to Idolatry**: Extreme nationalism arises when patriotism is misplaced, leading Christians to idolize their country and equate national success with divine favor. This idolatry shifts focus from God's sovereignty to a dangerous reverence for state power, contradicting the biblical command to seek first the Kingdom of God.

- **Consequences of National Superiority**: A belief in national superiority fosters a mindset that resists external influence and criticism, which can lead to conflicts and diminish international peace efforts. This sense of superiority is particularly harmful within the church, as it can hinder the Christian mandate to be peacemakers and global citizens of God's Kingdom.

- **Dangers of Tribalism and Insularity**: Within a nation, extreme nationalism promotes tribalism, dividing people into insular groups that see themselves as possessors of absolute truth. This division is not limited to national conflicts but extends into social and political realms, undermining unity and cooperation.

- **The Role of the Church in a Nationalistic Society**: The church must critically evaluate its role and influence in a nationalistic society. It should resist the temptation to align too closely with nationalistic agendas that compromise its global and kingdom-oriented mission.

- **Christian Response to Nationalism**: Christians are called to maintain a global perspective, recognizing their primary citizenship in the Kingdom of God. They should foster humility and openness, learning from diverse cultures and perspectives to enrich their understanding of God's multifaceted character.

Conclusion

"Patriotism Versus Extreme Nationalism" calls for

a careful distinction between healthy love for one's country and detrimental nationalism that opposes the Kingdom of God. Christians are encouraged to maintain their primary allegiance to God, ensuring their patriotism does not overshadow their identity as citizens of God's Kingdom. This balance is crucial for maintaining the integrity of the Christian witness in a world of diverse nations and cultures.

CHAPTER 9

GOD AND POLITICS

Bible Verse

Romans 12:2 (NKJV): "And do not be conformed to this world, but be transformed by the renewing of your mind, that you may prove what is that good and acceptable and perfect will of God."

Introduction

"God and Politics" explores the Christian's relationship with politics, emphasizing that true transformation in society is achieved through the power of God working through His people, rather than political means alone.

Word of Wisdom

"It is the power of God working through the people of God who bring true transformation." Emma Stark

Main Theme

The chapter challenges the effectiveness of political engagement in achieving spiritual and societal transformation, advocating for a focus on God's power and the mission of the church as the primary agents of change.

Key Points

• Initial political enthusiasm can lead to disillusionment about the impact of politics on societal change.

• True societal change is influenced by God through His people, not politics alone.

• Matthew 16 emphasizes the unique transformative power and authority given to the church.

• Political involvement can distract from the church's primary mission.

• The pursuit of political solutions can overshadow spiritual disciplines and kingdom-focused living.

Key Themes

• **Disillusionment with Politics**: Starting with a passion for political change, the narrative reveals a journey of disillusionment, where deeper societal issues seemed resistant to political solutions, leading to a realization that real change comes from spiritual transformation through the church.

- **The Role of the Church vs. Politics**:
  The chapter underscores the biblical view
  that the church, not political entities, is
  endowed with God's authority for societal
  transformation. This perspective shifts
  focus from political conquest to spiritual
  empowerment and kingdom-building.
- **Misconceptions of Success**: Success in
  Christian terms is often misconstrued as
  political influence or societal acceptance.
  However, true biblical success is depicted
  as resilience and faithfulness under societal
  rejection and spiritual opposition.
- **Righteousness Defined**: Righteousness
  in a nation is not about the dominance of
  Christian morality through law but the
  pervasive presence of genuine heart
  transformations that reflect Christ's
  lordship over individual lives.
- **Alternative Approaches to Societal
  Issues**: The chapter encourages Christians
  to think beyond legalistic solutions to
  societal issues, advocating for a more
  holistic approach that includes nurturing a
  culture of life and transformation that
  aligns with kingdom values.

Conclusion

"God and Politics" calls Christians to reevaluate
their engagement with politics, emphasizing that
the Kingdom of God operates on principles
distinct from worldly political systems. It
encourages a return to spiritual authority and
transformation as the true means to impact
societies, urging believers to prioritize their
spiritual identity over political affiliations.

CHAPTER 10

HOW GOD DISCIPLINES NATIONS

Bible Verse

Proverbs 14:34 (NIV): "Righteousness exalts a nation, but sin condemns any people."

Introduction

This chapter examines the role of culture in shaping politics and how God's discipline operates within nations. It challenges the belief that politics alone can lead to national righteousness, emphasizing instead the transformative power of God through His people.

Word of Wisdom

"It is the power of God working through the people of God who bring true transformation." Emma Stark

Main Theme

The chapter argues that true change in a nation comes not through political might or governance but through cultural transformation rooted in the righteousness and discipline of God.

Key Points

• Culture dictates politics, not the other way around.

• Nations receive leaders that reflect their cultural values and spiritual condition.

• Political changes alone cannot bring about righteousness in a nation.

• God uses rulers and historical events as tools for disciplining and shaping nations.

• True transformation occurs through the influence of a righteous remnant.

• The ultimate goal is not a righteous nation but a righteous people devoted to God.

Key Themes

• **Cultural Influence on Politics:** The chapter asserts that the culture of a people shapes their political landscape. A nation's politics are a reflection of its cultural values and norms, indicating that significant political change must begin with cultural transformation.

- **God's Sovereignty in Leadership:** It explores how God allows, and sometimes appoints, certain leaders to facilitate His divine purposes, including discipline. This selection is not always about endorsing the leaders' actions but about using them to accomplish broader divine objectives.
- **Role of Righteous Remnants:** The importance of a righteous remnant within a nation is highlighted. Such groups, though often small, are instrumental in steering their societies toward God's standards through their faith and actions, especially during periods of divine discipline.
- **Impact of Sin and Discipline:** The chapter discusses how God disciplines nations by letting them face the consequences of their sins, often through challenging leaders or oppressive regimes. This is meant to turn hearts back to Him and realign national priorities with His kingdom.
- **Misconceptions about Political Salvation:** A critical view is presented on the reliance on political systems to bring about spiritual renewal or salvation. It emphasizes that while governance can enforce law, it cannot transform hearts or impart righteousness.

Conclusion

The chapter concludes by urging believers to focus on cultivating personal and communal righteousness that influences culture. It calls for a reevaluation of expectations placed on political systems and a renewed commitment to living out the kingdom of God as the true solution to national and global issues.

CHAPTER 11

CULTURAL
PERSPECTIVES

Bible Verse

1 Peter 2:9 (NIV) - "But you are a chosen people, a royal priesthood, a holy nation, God's special possession, that you may declare the praises of him who called you out of darkness into his wonderful light."

Introduction

This chapter delves into how cultural backgrounds shape our views of the world, including our political and religious beliefs. It emphasizes the necessity of recognizing and questioning our culturally induced biases to truly follow Christ's teachings.

Word of Wisdom

"Your political opinion is influenced by your upbringing." Emma Stark

Main Theme

The influence of cultural perspectives on our understanding and engagement with the world, and the importance of aligning these views with the Kingdom of God rather than societal norms.

Key Points

• Culture dictates politics, not the other way around.

• Nations receive leaders that reflect their cultural values and spiritual condition.

• Political changes alone cannot bring about righteousness in a nation.

• God uses rulers and historical events as tools for disciplining and shaping nations.

• True transformation occurs through the influence of a righteous remnant.

• The ultimate goal is not a righteous nation but a righteous people devoted to God.

Key Themes

• **Cultural Influence on Politics:** The chapter asserts that the culture of a people shapes their political landscape. A nation's politics are a reflection of its cultural values and norms, indicating that significant political change must begin with cultural transformation.

- **God's Sovereignty in Leadership:** It explores how God allows, and sometimes appoints, certain leaders to facilitate His divine purposes, including discipline. This selection is not always about endorsing the leaders' actions but about using them to accomplish broader divine objectives.
- **Role of Righteous Remnants:** The importance of a righteous remnant within a nation is highlighted. Such groups, though often small, are instrumental in steering their societies toward God's standards through their faith and actions, especially during periods of divine discipline.
- **Impact of Sin and Discipline:** The chapter discusses how God disciplines nations by letting them face the consequences of their sins, often through challenging leaders or oppressive regimes. This is meant to turn hearts back to Him and realign national priorities with His kingdom.
- **Misconceptions about Political Salvation:** A critical view is presented on the reliance on political systems to bring about spiritual renewal or salvation. It emphasizes that while governance can enforce law, it cannot transform hearts or impart righteousness.

Conclusion

The chapter concludes by urging believers to focus on cultivating personal and communal righteousness that influences culture. It calls for a reevaluation of expectations placed on political systems and a renewed commitment to living out the kingdom of God as the true solution to national and global issues.

CHAPTER 12

WHOSE SIDE IS GOD ON?

Bible Verse

Romans 13:1 (NIV) - "Let everyone be subject to
the governing authorities, for there is no authority
except that which God has established. The
authorities that exist have been established by
God."

Introduction

This chapter challenges the common
notion that God supports any specific
political regime or system, emphasizing
that God's concern transcends human political
affiliations and focuses on higher divine
principles.

Word of Wisdom

*"We biblically fail when we assign God
to a side, or to a political party." Emma
Stark*

Main Theme

The chapter explores the neutrality of God in political matters, arguing that God does not align with any political system but works through them to achieve His purposes.

Key Points

• The Bible does not endorse any form of government as superior.

• God can work His purposes through any political system, including through flawed or corrupt means.

• True Christian allegiance transcends political affiliations, focusing instead on God's Kingdom.

• Biblical scripture encourages respect and submission to governing authorities as they are established by God.

• God's ultimate concern is for the spiritual maturity and readiness of His people, not political comfort.

• Prophetic voices should remain non-partisan to effectively communicate God's will.

Key Themes

• **Divine Neutrality in Politics:** The narrative stresses that God is not concerned with taking sides in human political disputes but is focused on ensuring that His divine will is accomplished through whatever means necessary. This includes using political systems that humans might deem corrupt or unjust.

- **Submission to Authority:** Echoing Romans 13, the chapter underscores the importance of respecting and submitting to governing authorities, recognizing them as God's instruments for maintaining order and executing justice, regardless of their flaws.

- **Prophetic Integrity:** It advocates for prophets to avoid political partisanship to maintain the purity of their message and ensure they represent God's voice and not personal or cultural biases. This impartiality allows them to effectively challenge and encourage the Church to align with God's commands.

- **The Danger of Political Idolatry:** Highlights the risk of Christians equating their political ideologies with divine endorsement, which can lead to idolatry and detract from the mission of the Church to advance the Kingdom of God.

- **Transformative Power of the Church:** Discusses the church's role in society, emphasizing that its power to effect change comes not from political alignment or influence, but from its unique position as the embodiment of God's Kingdom on Earth, tasked with living out and proclaiming the Gospel.

Conclusion

The chapter concludes by calling Christians to evaluate their political engagements through the lens of their primary allegiance to the Kingdom of God, urging them to seek divine guidance in their civic duties while maintaining a clear distinction between their spiritual commitments and their political opinions.

CHAPTER 13

HOW DO WE ACT NOW?

Bible Verse

Matthew 16:18 (NIV) - "...on this rock I will build
my church, and the gates of Hades will not
overcome it."

Introduction

This chapter explores the contrasting
biblical perspectives on influencing societal systems versus building the Kingdom
of God, challenging Christians to evaluate their
roles as either influencers within worldly systems or
builders of God's kingdom.

Word of Wisdom

*"We have become absolutely driven by
rising high and getting close to power."
Emma Stark*

Main Theme

The chapter discusses the effectiveness of Christians influencing secular systems versus actively building the Kingdom of God, using examples from both the Old and New Testaments to illustrate different models of societal transformation.

Key Points

• Biblical figures like Esther, Daniel, and Joseph exemplify the Old Testament model of gaining influence to enact change.

• The New Testament emphasizes building the Kingdom of God directly through spiritual transformation within individuals.

• Christians are called to build transformative systems outside of the world's systems, not just to integrate into them.

• Influencing societal systems often relies on reaching high positions of power to effect change.

• Building the Kingdom involves creating and leading new systems that align with God's values.

• The ultimate goal is not to dominate within existing worldly frameworks but to cultivate a distinct, God-centered community.

Key Themes

• **Contrast Between Old and New Testament Models:** The Old Testament model focuses on ascending within existing power structures to influence change, illustrated by figures like Esther and Daniel. In contrast, the New Testament advocates for a more foundational approach, emphasizing the building of the Kingdom of God from within individuals, spreading outwardly through genuine transformation rather than positional power.

- **Building vs. Influencing:** This theme delves into the practical differences between influencing from high societal positions and building new systems that inherently reflect Kingdom values. It questions the long-term effectiveness of merely influencing existing corrupt systems compared to establishing new structures based on biblical principles.
- **Role of Christians in Society:** The chapter encourages Christians to discern whether they are called to be influencers within worldly systems or builders of the Kingdom. It stresses the importance of understanding one's divine calling to effectively contribute to God's work on Earth.
- **Challenges of Political Engagement:** Discusses the complexities and potential pitfalls of Christians engaging in politics, warning against the idolatry of power and the misalignment of divine and political objectives. It emphasizes the need for a Kingdom-first approach, irrespective of political climates.

- **Strategic Building of the Kingdom:**
  Explores how Christians can practically
  build the Kingdom of God by establishing
  alternative systems such as education and
  media that reflect Christian values and
  serve the broader community, not just the
  church.

Conclusion

The chapter concludes with a call for Christians to
critically assess their impact on the world, whether
through positions of influence or through direct
Kingdom-building activities. It encourages a shift
from striving for earthly power to focusing on
spiritual growth and community transformation in
alignment with God's ultimate purposes.

CHAPTER 14

HOW DO YOU VOTE?

Bible Verse

Romans 14:7-8 NKJV - "For none of us lives to himself, and no one dies to himself. For if we live, we live to the Lord; and if we die, we die to the Lord. Therefore, whether we live or die, we are the Lord's."

Introduction

This chapter explores the spiritual responsibilities and considerations of Christians in the voting process, emphasizing the importance of seeking God's guidance over personal or cultural preferences.

Word of Wisdom

"The Kingdom of God grows amongst any political system." Emma Stark

Main Theme

The discussion focuses on the necessity for Christians to align their voting decisions with God's will, rather than succumbing to personal biases or societal pressures.

Key Points

• Christians are encouraged to consult the Holy Spirit when voting to ensure their choices align with God's will.

• Voting should transcend personal and cultural biases, focusing on God's larger plan.

• The concept of liberty is critically examined, highlighting the dangers of prioritizing personal freedom over moral accountability.

• The dangers of idolizing political systems and the notion of absolute freedom leading to moral anarchy are discussed.

• The chapter stresses the importance of understanding God's sovereignty over all forms of government and His ability to work through any system.

Key Themes

- **Spiritual Discernment in Voting:**
  Christians are urged to seek divine guidance at the ballot box, recognizing that God's perspective might differ from personal or popular opinions. This spiritual discernment helps align their choices with

God's broader objectives for justice and mercy.

- **Liberty and Idolatry:** The chapter critiques the idolization of liberty in Western cultures, pointing out that without a Christ-centered moral compass, liberty can lead to moral decay. It argues that true freedom is found in submission to Christ, not in the absence of moral constraints.

- **Sovereignty of God Over Political Systems:** It is emphasized that no political system is inherently more righteous or aligned with God's purposes. God's sovereignty means He can work through any system, whether democratic or authoritarian, to fulfill His purposes.

- **Impact of Cultural and Political Biases:** Voters are cautioned against allowing their cultural and political biases to cloud their judgment, highlighting the importance of viewing each vote as part of God's larger narrative rather than a pursuit of personal or nationalistic goals.

- **Role of Christians in Politics:** The text advises Christians involved in politics to maintain their allegiance to God over any political party or ideology. It emphasizes the importance of being a light in the political arena, advocating for God's justice and mercy without succumbing to partisan tactics.

Conclusion

The chapter concludes by reinforcing the need for Christians to prioritize God's kingdom and righteousness when voting. It calls for a heart and mind aligned with God's desires rather than worldly influences, ensuring that political engagement is an extension of one's faith commitment.

D DESTINY IMAGE

Destiny Image is a prophetic Christian publisher dedicated to empowering believers through Spirit-led messages. Our mission is to equip and inspire individuals to fulfill their God-given destinies by providing transformative resources that resonate with the Charismatic and Pentecostal faith.

We specialize in books, blogs, and back cover copies that reflect prophetic insights, dynamic teachings, and testimonies of faith. Our commitment to fostering spiritual growth and kingdom impact makes Destiny Image a beacon for those seeking to deepen their relationship with God and embrace their calling in the power of the Holy Spirit.